DOLPHIN TREASURE

D1495934

WAYNE GROVER

DOLPHIN TREASURE

ILLUSTRATED BY JIM FOWLER

 Harcourt

Orlando   Boston   Dallas   Chicago   San Diego

Visit *The Learning Site!*
www.harcourtschool.com

This edition is published by special arrangement with Morrow Junior Books,
a division of William Morrow & Company, Inc.

Grateful acknowledgment is made to Morrow Junior Books,
a division of William Morrow & Company, Inc. for permission to reprint
Dolphin Treasure by Wayne Grover, illustrated by Jim Fowler.
Text copyright © 1996 by Wayne Grover;
illustrations copyright © 1996 by Jim Fowler.

Printed in the United States of America

ISBN 0-15-314384-3

2 3 4 5 6 7 8 9 10   060   03 02 01 00

This story is dedicated to
the dolphins that must live
in concrete ponds
without freedom and without
the family structures they once had.

—W. G.

For Susi, who
values my dreams
and challenges me
to achieve them

—J. F.

Contents

□ C H A P T E R   O N E □

Sunken Spanish Treasure

I scanned the water in all directions, looking for my dolphin friend. Since I had saved his life by cutting a large fishhook from his tail when he was a baby, he had become my companion whenever I was at sea, diving or looking for old Spanish treasure on the seafloor.

Like a faithful and loving dog, Baby followed me

and my diving friends whenever we took our boat out to the clear water of the Atlantic Ocean, near Jupiter, Florida.

He and his dolphin family—mother, father, one brother, and two sisters—usually joined us as soon as we pulled out of the Jupiter Inlet, where the landlocked Intracoastal Waterway connects to the open sea.

I have no doubt that dolphins have good memories because within weeks after I had saved Baby's life, his family started following our boat whenever we sailed in the ocean.

Today Amos and I, along with Jack Riley, another diver, almost decided not to go looking for treasure at the site we had been working for several weeks. The weather looked threatening even though the sun broke through the clouds, making beautiful rays in the early dawn light.

Amos, at the wheel, knew the Florida weather better than anyone, and he didn't like what he was seeing as he steered the boat through the inlet and headed out

□   Sunken Spanish Treasure   □

to the open sea. He gunned the engines to attack the white-capped waves.

The outgoing tide of the inland waterway rushed to join the sea in a white-capped collision. Our thirty-four-foot boat, *Treasure Hunter*, was right in the middle of this treacherous area. Amos struggled to keep the boat from going up so steeply that it would flip over. We climbed the gigantic waves at the inlet's mouth until finally we cleared the area and entered the Atlantic.

It was early January, and the sea was rough. The wind sheared the wave tops off, forming little rainbows above each one as it marched shoreward. Through the early-morning mist I looked to see if dolphin fins were breaking the surface as the dolphins sped along, but there was none today.

Our diving site was off the coast three miles south of Jupiter. We were working to recover gold, silver, and jewels from an old Spanish treasure galleon that had sunk along with nine other ships during a hurricane in July 1715.

DOLPHIN TREASURE

The southeast coast of Florida is called the Treasure Coast for good reason. Along its shore lie the remains of dozens of Spanish treasure ships that were sunk over a three-hundred-year period. Many of them were caught in raging hurricanes that ripped them apart. Years of changing tides and storms had buried the ships. By using hand-held metal detectors that could locate objects hidden under the sand, Amos and I had discovered one of the old wrecks, and we were working to recover its treasure.

Baby had been at my side when I finally was able to ascertain the age of the old shipwreck we would be exploring again that day. I had been searching the seabed with a metal detector when suddenly I heard a loud whine in my earphone.

Baby responded with rapid clicks of excitement. He knew the sound meant I would stop to dig in the sand, and he loved to help.

As we swam slowly around, searching for metal, I was amazed to see an old anchor that weighed perhaps two tons, then another one. And nearby I saw a row

of cannon lying half buried in the sand. We had found the ship's final resting place.

I used my hand to clear the sand away from one of the cannon so I could see under it. It was slow going until Baby joined in. He became a dolphin digging machine. He hovered over the cannon and rapidly fluttered his big tail up and down, while holding himself stationary with his side flukes. Within seconds the cannon lay completely exposed. Baby watched me intently as I examined the encrusted cannon. Clicking like a sonar, he aimed his nose at the cannon as if to see for himself why I was so interested. When he clicked close to me, I could feel his sound waves hit my body. His sonar was better than the best ship's instrument.

On the underside of the cannon was a big clump of blackish material. I took a small hammer from my belt and hit it. It fell apart, spilling silver coins onto the sand.

I held one up and looked closely at it. On one side was a Spanish cross; on the other a royal shield with the date clearly visible: 1714. I looked at a second

Sunken Spanish Treasure

coin: 1713. I had found proof at last of the ship's identity. Our wreck was one of ten ships that had gone down in a hurricane on July 31, 1715. It could not have belonged to any other Spanish fleet because there was no record of any ships lost for several years before or after the 1715 tragedy.

Since that day Amos, Jack, and I, with Baby's help, had been searching to find the ship's treasure every chance we got. Because of the excitement of what we might discover next, we were going out on a winter day that looked less than perfect for diving.

As I stood holding on to the rail of the heaving boat, I kept looking for Baby, but neither he nor any other dolphins were in sight.

Amos was looking, too. "I guess Baby and his family are having a fresh fish breakfast somewhere out to sea," he said, smiling.

CHAPTER TWO

Baby, My Dolphin Companion

Finding the treasure had set our hearts pounding. Normally the treasure-diving season runs from April until late September, when the rough seas make anchoring the boat too difficult.

Amos, Jack, and I all have regular jobs because hunting for treasure is expensive, and even after it is discovered, by law the state of Florida gets 20 percent of the find. The treasure must be kept in a bank until the state, which has first choice, selects what it wants.

Unusually bad weather had prevented us from diving much during the summer so when there was a day that looked good even during winter, we sailed for the treasure site to work as long as the seas remained fairly calm.

Even if we don't get to dive, we all love being on the sea together, and it's a special treat when Baby and the other dolphins swim alongside our boat, jumping and frolicking, their perpetual smiles making us laugh.

Baby knows the sound of our engines, even though dozens of other boats are often in the area. He usually finds us just as we come out of the inlet. He follows close by the bow, riding the waves created by our boat.

Baby has become an eight-foot-long adult dolphin, a beautiful, sleek marine speed machine that can stay with our boat even when we race across the water.

He usually announces his arrival by coming up to the side of our boat, jumping high, and landing with a splash that wets us as we laugh and call his name.

Then he does a series of big arching jumps, splashing back into the water.

When we stop, he "tailwalks" right up to the boat. He stands up high above the water, fluttering his big tail to hold himself upright. He looks like a well-dressed waiter wearing a tuxedo and a big smile.

Baby loves to talk to me. He whistles, clicks, and grunts. He sometimes holds a sound for a long time, as if singing. When he does, I sing back to him. He seems to like my songs even though Amos and Jack don't exactly agree.

One day, as we sped toward the diving area, Baby, who was racing along next to us, suddenly made a sharp right turn and streaked away from the boat. After about fifty yards he turned and started back toward us, picking up speed until the water fanned out behind him. "What's that silly dolphin going to do? Ram us?" asked Amos.

We all watched Baby streak toward us. We were going at least thirty miles an hour, and he was coming right at us even faster. With a mighty leap Baby flew

over the boat and splashed into the water on the far side.

"Way to go, Baby," shouted Jack.

From that day on Baby made at least one jump over the boat when we pulled into the ocean from the inlet. He was telling us how happy he was to see us.

He often stays around for the entire day as we dive and work the treasure site. Then he accompanies us back as far as the inlet where the open ocean connects with the Intracoastal Waterway, its shore lined with marinas and buildings. Baby never enters the waterway. He is a creature wild and free, and the open ocean is his home. If he knew how many of his kind were trapped in small concrete ponds, forced to perform for sunburned tourists, I doubt that he would be quite so friendly toward us.

Baby learned early to answer to his name. If I call out something else, like "Hey, Charlie," to test him, he doesn't respond. Sometimes I call out a dozen names while he swims nearby, and he ignores them all until he hears "Baby." Then he rushes to the boat

Baby, My Dolphin Companion

and chatters as if to say, "Can't you remember my name?" When I want to call him while underwater, I tap three clicks on my diving tank with a rock or seashell from the ocean bottom, and usually Baby appears within a few minutes. His happy, smiling face makes even the grayest day seem bright.

Baby sometimes comes to visit us alone, but often he brings other family members to join us as we dive for treasure. We gave them all names because each one of them looks different, and they have different personalities. We call one Papa, one Mama, and one Goofy, because his dolphin "grin" is lopsided. We named Baby's sisters Angel and Bluebell. Another relative, with a huge shark bite scar, we call Old Scarback.

While the other dolphins swim along near the boat or watch us from afar as we work underwater, Baby always stays right with me, a member of the crew. Baby is so much a part of my life that even when I am not diving, I think of him often. It is as if we can communicate over a distance, or at least that's the way it seems to me.

DOLPHIN TREASURE

Baby was at my side watching my every move when I found the first gold from the old wreck. I was fanning the sand with my hand when a glint of metal caught my eye. It was a gold doubloon. I picked it up and looked at it carefully. Then I let out a bubbly "whoopee!" Baby felt my excitement and joined in with his dolphin clicking sounds. I think he was telling me he was happy, too.

Baby and I "talk" a lot underwater. As I breathe through my regulator, he loves to put his nose into the bubble stream rising to the surface. The bubbles must feel good to him because he spends a lot of time poking through them, sometimes chasing a favorite shiny one to the surface, where it breaks in the air.

The many treasure-laden shipwrecks left in the area by the Spaniards make for wonderful diving along the South Florida coast, especially when Amos, Jack, and Baby are along for company. It's sun, fun, and frustration sometimes, but it's always adventure. We have found only a few gold coins so far, but we know there is a king's ransom still there.

□ C H A P T E R   T H R E E □

Amos's Warning

Amos had been feeling poorly the last year, and I noticed he was more tired than normal.

By January Amos had had to give up diving altogether. Now he could only look on as Jack and I slipped into the clear water and slowly drifted down to the bottom without him. Jack and I work the equipment on the ocean floor, and Amos operates the boat above.

Today, with the wind rising and rainsqualls beating across the sea's surface, it looked as though we might have to call off the dive.

On the horizon huge swells were advancing one after the other. Somewhere out at sea a storm was churning, sending angry feelers all the way to our coastal beaches.

"I don't like the looks of those low clouds to the north," said Amos, peering over the boat's rising and falling bow. "There's a big rain coming, probably a good wind, too," he added.

"Amos, you're just getting old." Jack laughed. "We aren't going to let a little blow stop us from finding gold today, are we?"

"Jack, my boy, I've been sailing these seas since your mama was a little girl, and I've learned never to underestimate the Atlantic Ocean. When one of these winter squalls hits, it's like a freight train roaring down on you. One minute the sea is sunny and calm; the next the rain is pounding down, and the waves kick up to ten feet high or more."

Jack and I respect Amos, almost like a father. It's

hard not to like the old man. He looks like a Santa Claus, complete with white hair and beard. He's always laughing and joking, even when he feels bad.

"Well, then, we'd better start getting the anchors ready." Amos called over the sound of the twin Evinrude outboard engines pushing us along. "Wayne, check those ropes, we don't want to have the boat break loose and drift when you and Jack are on the bottom. With this strong current running, you'll never be able to get back aboard before I lose sight of you."

I looked at the sea passing beneath us as we climbed one swell after another. Amos steered the boat at forty-five degrees into each wave to keep from being pounded by rough water.

As the boat ran "uphill" into the swell, the engines strained tightly, and then, as we went down the back side, the props momentarily bit air instead of water and roared their protest at running at 100 percent power.

I loved it. The wind was cool on my face, and the seawater splashed over the side, wetting me from head

☐   Amos's Warning   ☐

to foot. I wondered if Baby and his family would join us on a stormy day like this as I looked for signs of dolphins in the rough sea.

They were nowhere to be seen. I looked from north to south, and except for a huge oil tanker out about five miles, we were alone on the sea. I felt the first tinge of uneasiness but didn't know why. Without Baby the day just would not be complete.

"How do you think those Spanish sailors felt as they sailed this area back in 1715?" asked Jack. "They had no engines, no radios, only a compass and sails. Can you imagine a one-hundred-forty-mile-per-hour wind shrieking through the rigging, toppling masts and ripping sails to shreds? Those guys were real sailors.

"Look around. We're the only ones at sea today. Everybody else is home watching TV or shopping at the malls. I say, let's dive and get treasure."

Amos smiled through his stained beard, his missing back teeth showing clearly. "Jack, if you and Wayne want adventure, then you shall have it. I was just about to say it's too dangerous and turn back, but then I remembered how we used to ride out the big storms at sea and laugh at them. You're right. We've become too soft and civilized.''

It was clear to me that Amos was feeling his best days were behind him and he wanted to capture one more great adventure.

I watched the shore carefully, finally locating the marks we used to triangulate our extact position. We were using a loran electronic location device to get pretty near the spot, but it had an error margin of about a quarter mile.

We had thought about keeping a floating marker over our salvage site, but it would only invite others to steal what we had worked so hard to uncover. Our treasure site was in seventy feet of water, requiring us to keep a close watch on our bottom time. This was to prevent us from getting the bends caused by too much nitrogen in our body tissues, which could result in paralysis and even death.

We would be able to stay down forty-five minutes the first dive, rest on the surface for an hour, and dive for another thirty-five minutes.

Gold and Jewels

"This is it. Drop anchor," called Amos. Jack let the bow anchor drop with a splash. It had to go down seventy feet and be dragged in the sand until its flukes bit and held. We needed the *Treasure Hunter* to be right over the wreck site.

Because the running sea could swing the boat back and forth, we also had to set two stern anchors, one from the port side and one from the starboard side. Once we had all three anchors set, we used a hydraulic pulley to drag the boat between the two stern anchors until it sat directly above the site.

With the anchors holding, the boat stayed pretty much in the same spot. We dropped down a big air pressure–operated vacuum, called an air lift, to suck sand from the wreck site. It works by air being pumped through a small tube along the six-inch flexible hose line to create a vacuum at the nozzle.

It is always a lot of hard work to stabilize the boat, get the equipment in place, and then dive with the metal detectors to locate the areas from which we want to vacuum the sand.

Today, with the high swells running, getting the anchors set and the air lift down was harder than usual. I began to wonder if we had not let our spirit of adventure overcome our common sense.

Finally we had all three anchors set. Jack and I put on our wet suits, pulled on our scuba tanks, adjusted our lead weight belts, and sat down, facing each other on opposite sides of the boat.

☐ Gold and Jewels ☐

I gave a thumbs-up sign that I was ready to go. Jack smiled, put his mouthpiece in, and returned the sign. I dropped backward into the sea off the starboard side. Jack went in from the port side.

As soon as I hit the water, I pointed head down, kicked my fins, and started for the bottom. I looked over to my left and saw Jack diving straight down, streaming a trail of bubbles from his regulator.

Down, down we went until the ocean floor came into view. The visibility was good as we leveled off over the place where the cannon were lying side by side, just as they had been since 1715. The huge air lift pipe was rising and falling as the boat above went up and down in the swells.

The last time we had worked the site, I had found a hot spot that made the metal detectors sing our favorite song. As soon as we got the air lift nozzle in place, Jack held it over the sand and turned on the handle that let compressed air from the boat above blast down and create a vacuum effect.

Sand and small objects were sucked up into the hose and deposited on a wire mesh catcher screen on the boat's rear deck, where Amos was watching for anything that might be valuable. Jack and I looked on as the sand was lifted away and the hole grew deeper.

With the sand rising into the hose, I examined every clump that was uncovered. There were ancient fossilized seashells of every size, slowly wearing down over the centuries to become sand. Dark rocks came into view, and I held them close to my face mask to see if

□ Gold and Jewels □

they were artifacts or coin clusters. They were only rocks and more rocks.

It was truly a treasure hunt. The next moment we might find silver or gold—or perhaps nothing.

For twenty-five minutes we scoured the area, stopping to use the detector to be sure it still indicated metal somewhere under the sand. Suddenly the whine rose in intensity when I placed the detector loop on the sand.

I missed Baby's curious eyes watching my every move. It just was not the same without him. The whine grew louder and louder. There had to be something down there! Jack turned on the air lift again and moved the nozzle back and forth, causing the sand to rise into it like a small tornado. Then I saw a glint of metal and immediately reached over and shut off the suction.

Jack saw it, too. We hand fanned the bottom where we saw the glint, but the sand caved into the hole and covered it. We both continued to fan carefully, stopping to stick our fingers into the soft sand to feel for an object.

I checked my watch. Thirty minutes had passed, and

my air supply gauge indicated five hundred pounds left. It was time to surface. Jack glanced at his air gauge, then looked at me and made a throat-cutting motion. He was nearly out of air.

Just at that moment a gold chain with large carved links came into view in the sand. I fanned around it, slipped my left hand under it, and pulled gently to remove it from its 277-year-old grave. The long chain came out slowly, inch by inch, for about two feet. Then it caught tight.

Jack's air tank went dry. His chest heaved to suck air, but there was none. He had to go to the surface . . . *now!*

I tried once more to pull the chain loose, but it was lodged tight. I let it go and helped Jack.

I drew a long breath from my mouthpiece, took it out, and gave it to Jack. He put it into his mouth and drew deeply three times, then gave it back to me.

We started toward the surface seventy feet above, face-to-face, sharing my limited air supply. It seemed to take forever, but within a minute or so we were safe.

We broke the surface about twenty feet from the boat. A heavy rain was pelting down, making millions of small splashes as it hit right under our noses.

I looked at the boat and saw Amos waving his arms madly. I couldn't wait to tell him what we had found. We swam over and climbed the ladder to the deck, smiling from ear to ear.

Before I could speak, Amos said, "We've got to pull anchor and get to shelter. There's a marine weather warning of strong squalls moving over us, and a waterspout has been sighted. Let's move!"

"Amos, wait a minute. We found gold! There's a large chain down there. I uncovered about two feet of it, but it's stuck. I want to go back down and get it. It could be the biggest find yet."

"That's right, Pop!" exclaimed Jack. "That chain must weigh five pounds. It's worth a fortune!"

"Whoa, partners. Look at that squall coming right at us," said Amos. "The radio says the waves may be up to fifteen feet in the squall line. Gold or no gold, we've got to haul up and haul out."

Gold and Jewels

Jack and I looked at the black wall of water rapidly approaching from the northeast. It looked pretty grim, with lightning and the sound of thunder rolling across the waves.

"Look, Amos, you and Jack start hauling the anchors, and I'll put on a fresh tank and go back down to free the chain. By the time you get the two stern lines freed, I'll be back with the gold."

"Wayne, that's a very bad idea. If the bowline snaps, we'll be unable to hold position. If you miss the boat, we'll never find you. And it's five miles to shore."

"Amos, you're right, but you didn't see that gold chain. It has huge links, each carved with little flowers. It's got to be from a treasure chest," Jack argued, already winding the port anchor rope around the pulley.

We respected Amos's assessment of the conditions, but we had worked two years to find the main treasure area of the wreck site. Still, if he said no, we would abide by his decision.

Lost in a Stormy Sea

The boat strained against its anchor lines, rising and falling as the waves crashed by. The anchors had to be released before the ropes broke. The wind was roaring, and the driving rain stung our faces. It was now or never.

"Okay, Wayne. I'll give you five minutes, no more. We have to get to shelter before we lose the boat and all end up in the water."

☐　Lost in a Stormy Sea　☐

"Okay, Amos, five minutes. I can do it."

I quickly slipped a full tank into my backpack and turned on the air. As I stepped to the rail, Jack and Amos were ready to haul in the two stern achors. I had to hurry.

Holding my face mask with my right hand, I jumped feetfirst into the water. Flipping over and kicking powerfully with my swim fins, I dived straight to the bottom. I could feel the sea's surges even down past forty feet as I headed back to the place where we had found the gold chain.

From the corner of my eye I saw the big air lift pipe jerking upward as Jack and Amos hurriedly pulled it to the boat.

There it was. The chain lay like a gold snake coiled on the seabed. I settled over it and started working my fingers down into the sand, feeling the chain between my thumb and fingers. Deeper and deeper I probed. There seemed to be no end. It was a race against time.

I knew that the scene above on the boat would be chaos about now. I had to free the chain and get back before the huge waves ripped the boat from the site.

This is stupid, I told myself. I've let gold fever override my better sense. What if I get stuck alone at sea in this raging storm?

I worked feverishly, waving sand away while pulling at the chain. I looked at my watch. Four minutes had gone by.

From the corner of my eye, I saw the starboard anchor rope come snaking down and fall nearby. Its frazzled end told the tale. It had parted, snapped by the raging seas.

That meant the boat would not be where I left it.

Okay, Wayne, I scolded myself. It's time to give up and get out of here.

Just then my fingers touched something on the chain that was different. I dug deeper into the sand until I was in up to my elbows. I worked the chain, and it came loose. I pulled it up inch by inch with both hands.

As it cleared the sand, I saw a large gold crucifix, studded with red stones. Rubies! I thought. The chain was about four feet long. It was incredibly beautiful.

My heart pounded with excitement as I wrapped the

whole chain around my left arm and pulled the cross close to my face mask. It was at least four inches high and studded with red stones. The chain had diamonds fixed in every fifth link.

At that moment I knew we had found part of the treasure that had probably been kept in a chest in the captain's cabin. There might even be part of the chest itself deeper in the sand.

I was quickly making sure there was no more gold in the hole when my fingers touched another chain. I frantically worked to free it, but my time was up. I had to surface.

As I climbed up, I could both see and feel the huge waves that lashed the sea above. By the time I reached ten feet from the surface, the surge was so powerful my body was being slung back and forth as the waves passed overhead.

My head broke the surface. The boat was gone. I spun in a circle, and there, to the west, was the *Treasure Hunter* being swept shoreward. I guessed in an instant what had happened.

Lost in a Stormy Sea

When the stern line broke, the bowline had held long enough for the boat to be pulled down when a big wave rolled by. Instead of climbing up the wave, the anchor held the boat down, and the wave broke right over it, flooding the engines. Amos had been forced to cut the bowline to keep the boat from sinking.

I could see him and Jack desperately working on the engines, trying to start them, but with every passing second, the boat moved farther from me. When a huge wave passed under me and I was at its peak, I saw Jack looking for me.

I waved frantically.

But by the time I slid down the back side of the wave and rose on the next one, I was alone. The boat was nowhere to be seen.

"Amos!" I shouted. My voice was swallowed by the raging storm. I strained to see the boat, but with the pouring rain and waves breaking all around me, it was impossible.

I hit the inflate button on my buoyancy compensator (BC), and the air filled it until I was floating in the squall-

lashed water. I looked at the beautiful chain and crucifix wrapped around my arm and smiled. It was solid gold and was studded with diamonds and rubies. But now I had real problems.

I was lost and alone in a storm-tossed sea. Even if Amos and Jack got the boat's engines started, they would never find me, and they had to get the boat to sheltered water immediately.

I have been diving most of my adult life and have faced some pretty scary moments at sea, but this one was the worst. To swim to shore, five miles to the west, was possible, but I was in the Gulf Stream, which ran north at about six miles an hour, taking anything and everything with it. I remembered hearing of fishing boats breaking down off the Palm Beach area and drifting all the way to the Georgia coast before being found.

Okay, Wayne. Stay calm! You're still strong and can float with the current. The water is warm, and when the storm is over, the Coast Guard will be looking for you. I tried to convince myself.

I looked at my watch. It was 12:25 P.M., but the

☐ Lost in a Stormy Sea ☐

storm clouds were so black it was like night. A chill ran through me. I was colder than I should have been.

Hypothermia!

Because I had been on the cold bottom, my body temperature had dropped. I knew I had to stay warm or I could die of exposure.

The rain was so heavy I could not tell where the shore was. Usually the condos that line the South Florida beaches stand out like white sentinels, marking the shoreline, but I could see nothing.

I started swimming, kicking my fins for propulsion, but I realized immediately that the waves were so high and the current so strong I could make no headway or even stay on a straight course as I swam.

I'd better wait for the storm to pass before I waste all my energy, I reasoned. Better to end up somewhere to the north than to drown trying to fight the waves.

Each passing wave slapped me in the face, causing me to swallow salt water if I didn't react in time. Because snorkels interfere with working on the bottom, I was not wearing one. A snorkel would have allowed me to float facedown and rise and fall with the waves as I breathed above them. I wished I had one.

For hours I floated, fighting to breathe and trying to see the shoreline so I could save myself. I had no idea if Amos and Jack had made it to safety.

Night came about 5:30 P.M., and the storm was still raging.

While it was still light, I had felt pretty confident I could survive, but after nightfall, alone, tired, and cold, I realized this might be my last day on earth.

And for what? I scolded myself. A gold anchor to help me sink to the bottom.

By midnight I was totally exhausted. I had dropped my weight belt and tank about an hour after I surfaced. All I had in the world now was my BC, my fins, and a gold chain with a ruby-studded crucifix meant for the king of Spain. Even my diving mask had been ripped from my face by the surging waves.

I was so tired I could barely move. My legs kept cramping until finally I was forced to kick off my swim

Lost in a Stormy Sea

fins, despite the fact that without them I would have to swim unaided for many miles.

By 3:00 A.M. I was shaking with cold and riding lower in the water. I realized my BC had lost air pressure. I was sinking fast.

DOLPHIN TREASURE

With no tank to bleed air from, I used the manual mouthpiece to reinflate it: my only hope now. The air went out as fast as I blew it in. I saw bubbles coming from a worn-looking hole in the fabric. The constant motion of the rising and falling waves had chafed it until it leaked air. Now I was in real trouble.

During the last hours the sea had moderated until the waves were only about five feet high, but for my exhausted body, they may as well have been a hundred feet.

Lost in a Stormy Sea

Treading water with my last reserves of energy, I slipped out of my BC, which was now just a useless weight. Only my thin rubber diving suit was between me and the sea.

I can make it, I thought. I had to have faith that somehow I would be saved, but in reality I knew I stood very little chance of surviving.

Suddenly something brushed my legs, and I jerked them away. The adrenaline rushed to my heart. I knew what it was: sharks!

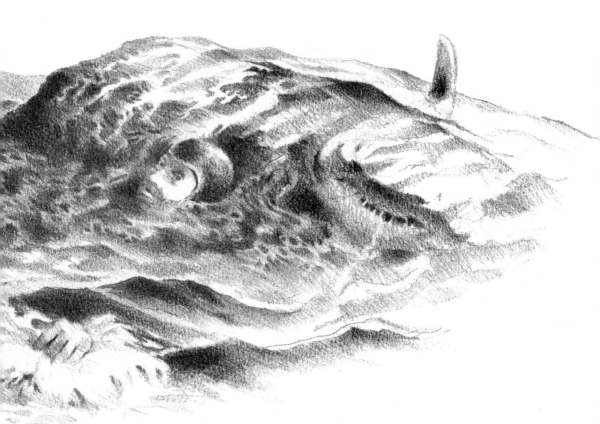

Sharks feed at night and will attack anything they can eat without a fight. I splashed with my arms and kicked my feet. My heart nearly stopped when my hand hit the rough sandpaper hide just inches from me.

I had dived around sharks for years and had no fear of them. But being on the surface at night, alone and barely moving, I was an inviting dinner, and I knew it. I was about to be eaten by a shark because I had let a gold crucifix and chain cloud my judgment.

Bump! This time I was hit harder.

I knew the shark was sizing me up for a meal. I had no way to defend myself, not even a diving knife. It was onboard the boat, useless to me now.

Then: stillness. I spun around, trying to see in the dark, but it was as black as pitch. Anguish swept over me. With my right hand I touched the heavy chain still wrapped around my left arm. My nearly total fatigue made it feel like a weight pulling me straight to the bottom. Why hadn't I let it go along with my diving gear earlier?

Lost in a Stormy Sea

   I unwrapped the heavy chain from around my arm, opened my fingers wide, and let it slowly slide downward, back to the seabed where it had lain since that stormy day back in 1715.

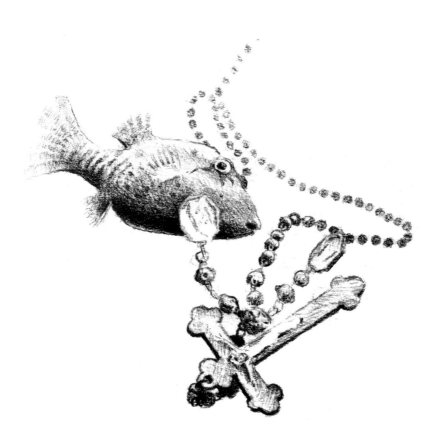

CHAPTER SIX

Baby Saves My Life

"Help me!" I shouted into the blackness, knowing there was no one to hear. "Someone, please help me!" Again and again I shouted.

Bump! Bump!

This is it, I thought. The last bump before the bite.

I wondered how long it took to die when a shark bit into you. I was almost too exhausted to care.

Baby Saves My Life

Suddenly the water near me erupted in an audible WHOMP! as something was hit hard.

WHOMP!—again and then again!

Then I heard the sweetest sound I'll ever hear. It was the chatter of a dolphin, a high-pitched musical note that brought tears to my eyes. Right under my nose a large warm body rose from the water and blew a sharp spout of warm air from its blowhole. It was a big dolphin.

I wrapped one arm around its broad back and held on to its dorsal fin.

"Is that you, Baby?" I whispered.

The dolphin chattered and raised its bottle nose three times in quick succession.

With my other hand I felt near the tail. The scar was easily discernible. Close by I heard other dolphins chattering their greetings. Baby had brought his whole family to me.

"Thank you, God," I said quietly.

At least I was not going to die alone, eaten by sharks. Baby chattered at me and kept raising his bottle nose up under my arm, like a dog wanting to be petted. I was so near total exhaustion I could hardly move my arms, but I managed to lay them both over his back and use his body as a float while I rested.

I had heard old sailors' stories about dolphins' rescuing men from the sea, but I had never believed them. Yet here I was, moments from death, and dolphins had come to help me.

□ Baby Saves My Life □

Baby chirped and began slowly swimming, forcing me to grab on to his dorsal fin with both hands as he dragged me through the water. He could swim thirty miles an hour, yet he was barely moving, gently pulling me through the darkness. He sensed I was near the end of my strength.

I slipped off and grabbed for his fin. I slipped off again. I was so tired my hands were too weak to hold on against the pressure of the water against my body. Baby chattered with a high-pitched singsong sound. Another dolphin answered.

From behind, it slid its head under my trailing torso and lifted me onto its back. When it breathed, a fishy-smelling vapor wafted up into my face.

The two dolphins held me up. Baby dragged me, and the other dolphin pushed me along through the water. I didn't know if we were headed for the open sea or toward shore, but I was so exhausted and relieved I didn't care.

"Baby, I love you," I said as I struggled to stay on top of the slippery dolphin. A sharp breath exhalation and several chirps from Baby let me know he was listening and answering in his own way.

Hour after hour Baby and the other dolphin moved me through the water. As the first rays of light came out of the east, I could see I was in the middle of a school of dolphins, not just Baby's immediate family.

The dolphin holding me up from behind was a male even bigger than Baby. It was Papa, who had saved us both from sharks years before.

I tried to convince myself that I was alive and not dreaming. I counted the dolphins that surrounded me like a ring of guardian angels. There were fifteen.

As the sun rose, I could see the shoreline in the distance. The storm had passed, and the sea was almost calm again.

I had drifted off to sleep for a few moments as the warmth of Baby and the other dolphins brought back some of my strength. I started to slip off. When I did, Papa nudged me sharply as if to say, "Hold on. Stay awake."

When we were about a mile from shore, I could see buildings clearly. The sun was warming my back now, and I felt new energy. I was very thirsty and hungry, but I was safe.

I kept thinking, Who will ever believe this?

I didn't quite believe it myself, yet it was happening.

I was sure my wife thought me dead by now.

Far to the south I saw several boats out at sea. It was probably the Coast Guard looking for me and perhaps for Amos and Jack, too. What if I had caused the deaths of my two dear friends?

We came closer and closer to shore until I could hear the surf breaking. The dolphins brought me up

☐ Baby Saves My Life ☐

to the beach near a tall condo, bathed in the golden early-morning sunlight.

Then Papa backed off, and my legs dropped down. My feet touched the ground. I was safe. Baby chirped repeatedly and kept raising his nose. I let go of his fin, and he made a noise that sounded like a fast, high laugh.

All the dolphins joined in the chorus. I stood with tears of joy in my eyes as my rescuers cavorted in the shallow water. They rushed back and forth and slapped the water with their tails. It was like a beach party with a lot of good friends.

One by one they left and went back to deeper water. Baby was the last to go. He floated by my side, chirping and blowing his fishy breath out in little puffs of vapor.

"Thank you, Baby. Thank you for saving my life."

He floated close to me and chattered his happy dolphin song. I owed him my life, which I had foolishly endangered for a golden chain.

He turned, swam toward the open sea, and dived out of sight. Suddenly he broke the surface in a high arch that took him several feet above the water. He hit with a big splash and did it again. He was saying good-bye.

"Good-bye, Baby," I called out.

I walked up the beach and crossed to the wooden stairs of a nearby condo. It was 7:27 A.M. on January 9, and I was alive.

After a lady wearing a housecoat got over the shock of seeing a tired man wearing a sand-covered black rubber suit at her door, she let me in to use the phone.

"Honey, I'm alive. I'm okay."

My wife cried, "Oh, Wayne! I never gave up hope. Amos and Jack came to see me last night to give me the bad news. But in my heart I knew you would make it safely. Tell me . . . what happened?"

I took a breath and said, "Honey, you'll never believe it."

WAYNE GROVER was born in Minneapolis, Minnesota. He is a veteran of the United States Air Force and has traveled the world during and after his twenty-five-year military career. He is an active conservationist and an avid parachutist, a scuba diver, white-water rafter, hiker, and naturalist. He has worked on shark research in the Pacific, and at present his chief interests are marine research and historical wrecks.

Now a freelance journalist, his articles on conservation and ecological balance have appeared in newspapers and magazines throughout the world.

He is the author of *Ali and the Golden Eagle* and *Dolphin Adventure*. He lives with his wife, Barbara, in Florida.

JIM FOWLER grew up in Tulsa, Oklahoma, and moved to Alaska in 1973. He enjoys kayaking, camping, and wildlife viewing. He is the illustrator of *I'll See You When the Moon Is Full, When Joel Comes Home*, and *Fog*, all by Susi Gregg Fowler, and of *Dolphin Adventure* by Wayne Grover.

The Fowlers live in Juneau, Alaska, with their daughters, Angela and Micaela.